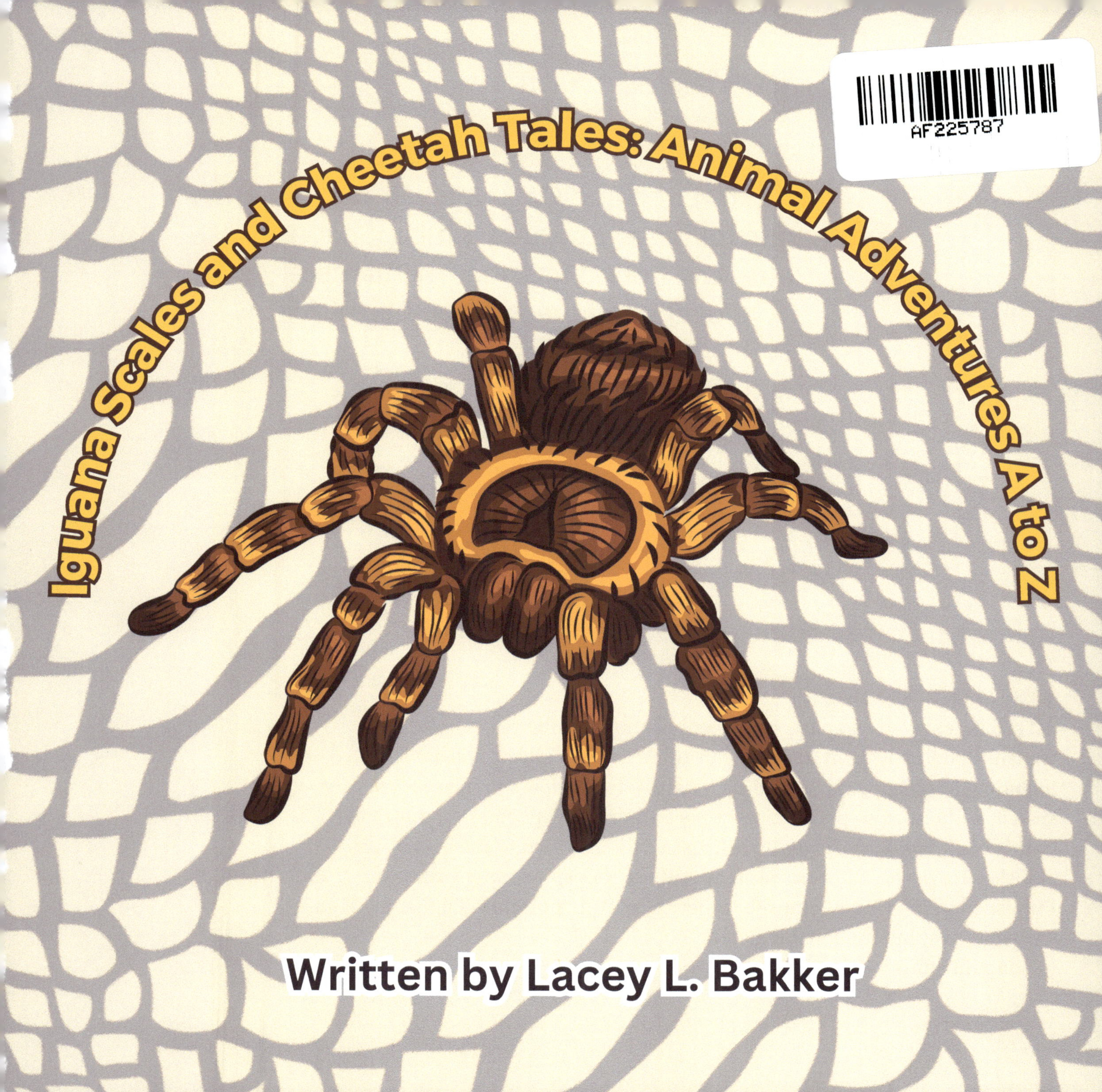

Iguana Scales and Cheetah Tales: Animal Adventures A to Z
Written by Lacey L. Bakker

For Luna and Octo-Miss Prime
and in loving memory of Simba, Seabass,
Bella, and John McClane (the hamster,
not the beloved action hero)
 Mum

ISBN: 978-1-989506-97-4

Answers to back cover: Lion, Habitat, Endangered, Cheetah, Forest

This book belongs to:

A is for Armadillo. Armadillos are small mammals known for their armored shells which are made up of bony external plates overlaid with scales. The body is flexible, with softer skin underneath that helps to expand and contract. They are native to the Americas and are primarily nocturnal, feeding on insects and small invertebrates. Armadillos can roll themselves into a tight ball when threatened, providing protection for their soft underbelly.

B is for **Bear**. Bears are large mammals found across various habitats worldwide. They are known for their powerful build, sharp claws, and omnivorous diet. Species include the polar bear, brown bear, and black bear. Bears have an exceptional sense of smell, which they use to locate food sources from miles away.

C is for **Cheetah**. Cheetahs are the fastest land animals, capable of reaching speeds up to 60-70 miles per hour in short bursts. Their tail acts like a rudder on a boat, allowing the cheetah to make quick and precise turns while chasing prey. Cheetahs have unique tear marks running from the inside corners of their eyes to the outside edges of their mouth, helping to reduce glare from the sun while hunting.

D is for **Dolphin.** Dolphins are highly intelligent marine mammals known for their playful behavior and social nature. They are found in oceans and seas around the world. Dolphins use a technique called echolocation to navigate and locate prey underwater by emitting high-pitched sounds and interpreting the echoes that bounce back.

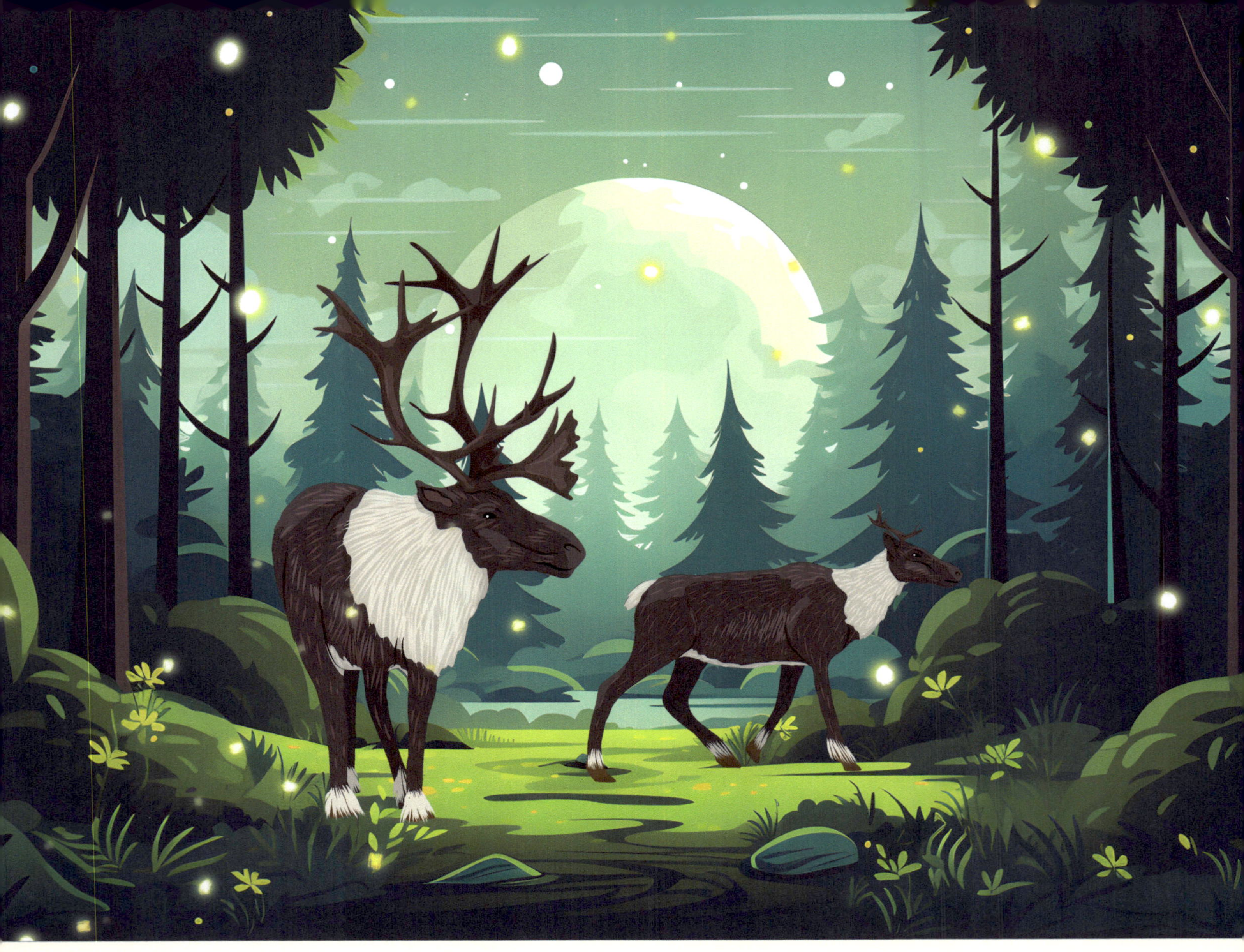

E is for **Elk**. Elks are large members of the deer family found in North America and parts of Asia. They are known for their impressive antlers, which are shed and regrown annually by males. Elks inhabit forests, grasslands, and mountainous regions, and feed on grasses, leaves, and twigs. Elks are excellent swimmers and can cross rivers and lakes to reach new feeding areas or escape predators.

F is for **Fox.** Foxes are small to medium-sized animals that belong to the same family as dogs, wolves, coyotes, and jackals. They are known for their cunning nature, bushy tails, and nocturnal habits. Species include the red fox, arctic fox, and fennec fox. Foxes have excellent hearing and can locate small prey underground by using their sensitive ears to detect movement.

G is for **Giraffe.** Giraffes are the world's tallest land animals, known for their long necks and spotted coats. They inhabit savannas, grasslands, and open woodlands in Africa and are herbivores, primarily feeding on leaves from tall trees. Giraffes have extremely long tongues, measuring up to 18 inches in length, which they use to grasp leaves and twigs from high branches.

H is for **Hyena.** Hyenas are carnivorous mammals found in Africa and parts of Asia. They are known for their distinctive vocalizations, scavenging behavior, and powerful jaws capable of crushing bones. Hyenas live in savannas, forests, and deserts, and are skilled hunters as well as scavengers. Hyenas have a stronger biteforce than lions!

I is for **Iguana.** Iguanas are large lizards known for their long tails, spiny crests along their backs, and ability to change color for thermoregulation. If threatened, an iguana can detach its tail, distracting the predator while the iguana makes its escape. Eventually the tail will regrow, but the new tail may not be as long as the original. Iguana scales have tiny sensory cells that can detect even the slightest vibrations in their environment alerting them to predators.

J is for **Jellyfish.** Jellyfish are fascinating marine creatures found in oceans worldwide. They come in a variety of shapes, sizes, and colors. Jellyfish have soft, gelatinous bodies and tentacles armed with stinging cells called nematocysts, which they use to capture prey and defend against predators. Jellyfish existed *before* dinosaurs and are the oldest multi-organed animals on Earth!

K is for **Komodo Dragon**. Komodo dragons are the largest living lizards in the world, found in the Indonesian islands of Komodo, Rinca, Flores, and Gili Motang. They're fierce predators, equipped with strong jaws and sharp teeth. They have a venomous bite, capable of immobilizing their prey. Once bitten, their victims weaken from the venom before becoming the dragon's meal.

L is for **Lion**. Lions are symbols of strength and majesty, known for their loud and deep roars that can be heard up to 5 miles away. They live in groups called prides consisting of related females and their babies, as well as a few males. Within the pride, lionesses are the primary hunters, working together to stalk and ambush prey. Lions spend up to 20 hours a day sleeping to conserve energy for hunting and protecting their territory.

M is for **Meerkat**. Meerkats belong to the mongoose family, found in southern Africa. They live in groups called mobs or gangs, typically consisting of around 20 individuals. They have excellent vision and a strong sense of smell, which they use to detect predators and locate food. Meerkats take turns acting as guards keeping watch for predators while the rest of the group forages for food.

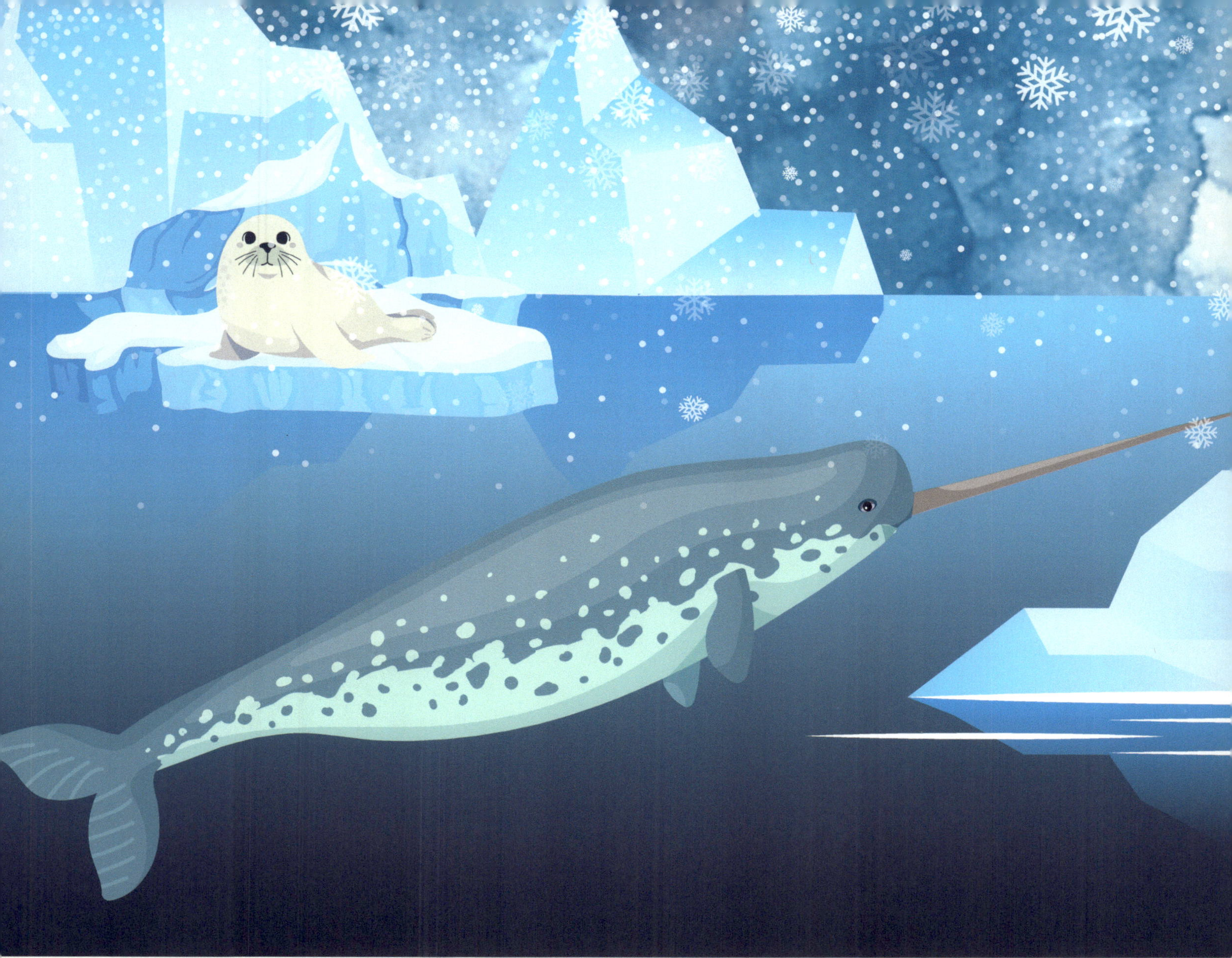

N is for **Narwhal.** Narwhals are medium-sized whales found in Arctic waters. They are known for the long, spiral tusks protruding from their heads, which can grow up to 10 feet long in males. Narwhal's tusks are actually elongated teeth, with some individuals having two tusks, and they are used for various purposes, including navigation, communication, and hunting.

O is for **Orangutan.** Orangutans are large apes native to the rainforests of Borneo and Sumatra. They are known for their red fur, long arms, and gentle demeanor. Orangutans are critically endangered due to habitat destruction and poaching. Orangutans have the longest inter-birth interval of any mammal, with females typically giving birth only once every 6 to 8 years.

P is for **Penguin.** Penguins have flipper-like wings and torpedo-shaped bodies, which allow them to swim with agility underwater. They have adapted to live in some of the coldest places on Earth! Penguins have a gland near their tails that secretes an oil that they spread over their feathers to waterproof them, helping them stay warm and buoyant in the cold ocean waters.

Q is for **Quail.** Quail feathers are earthy tones such as brown, gray, and tan, which provide excellent camouflage against their natural habitats. Male quails have more vibrant feathers compared to females. Quails, may use various cues such as the sun, stars, landmarks, and even Earth's magnetic field to navigate during migration.

R is for **Ram** A ram's horns can weigh up to 30 pounds and continue to grow throughout its life. Found in mountainous regions and grasslands worldwide, these majestic animals possess a keen sense of smell, aiding them in detecting predators and locating food sources. With their excellent climbing abilities, they easily navigate steep and rocky terrains.

S is for **Shark.** Sharks are apex predators found in oceans around the world. Sharks, like the great white, have an impressive sense of smell. They can detect blood in the water measured in parts per million or even parts per billion. Certain sharks, such as the great white, may sense blood from several miles away.

T is for **Tarantula**. Tarantulas are found in habitats around the world, including deserts, forests, and grasslands. Most tarantula species are not venomous to humans. Tarantulas molt (shed) their exoskeleton as they grow. Before molting, tarantulas stop eating and become less active. After shedding their old exoskeleton, they emerge with a soft, vulnerable new exoskeleton that gradually hardens over time.

U is for **Urutú**. Urutú are venomous pit vipers found in South America and are capable swimmers. Regarding reproduction, female Urutús retain eggs inside her body until they hatch, and then she gives birth to fully developed young.

V is for **Vulture**. Vultures are found on every continent except Antarctica. Vultures clean up decaying animal carcasses (carrion) and their stomach acid has a pH level close to battery acid. This allows them to safely consume carrion infected with bacteria and pathogens.

W is for **Wolf**. Wolves are found worldwide and are apex predators. Wolves can smell a dead moose or caribou buried under ten feet of snow, even if the wind is blowing in the wrong direction. A typical wolf pack consists of 6 to 10 wolves such as the alpha male and alpha female, their babies, and other related or unrelated wolves.

X is for **Xenops**. Xenops are small, insect-eating birds found in Central and South America. They have long, slender bills and short tails, and they forage for insects and larvae in the bark and foliage of trees. The male and female birds collaborate closely during the incubation period of their babies, with each taking shifts to ensure that the eggs are kept warm and protected from potential threats.

Y is for **Yak**. Yaks are native to the Himalayan region of Asia. They are well adapted to high-altitude environments, with thick fur, large lungs, and hooves designed for traveling rugged terrain. Unlike the hooves of many other animals, which are flat, yak hooves have a concave shape with sharp edges. This unique design provides excellent traction on rocky slopes and slippery surfaces.

Z is for **Zebra**. Underneath those striking black and white patterns, zebras have dark skin! Zebra's stripes help with camouflage, temperature regulation, and discouraging biting flies. Their stripes create an optical illusion which confuses predators and makes it more difficult for them to accurately judge the zebra's speed and direction of movement.

Glossary of Words

1. **Omnivorous:** an animal that eats both plants and animals.
2. **Echolocation:** the ability of certain animals to locate objects by emitting sound waves and understanding the echoes they receive.
3. **Nocturnal:** referring to animals that are active during the night.
4. **Carnivorous:** an animal that primarily eats meat.
5. **Herbivore:** an animal that primarily eats plants.
6. **Thermoregulation:** the ability of an organism to regulate its body temperature.
7. **Nematocysts:** specialized stinging cells found in cnidarians such as jellyfish, used for defense and capturing prey.
8. **Navigation:** the process of determining and maintaining a course or direction while traveling.
9. **Poaching:** the illegal hunting or capturing of wild animals, typically for commercial gain.
10. **Buoyant:** able to float or rise in a fluid; having positive buoyancy.
11. **Migration:** the seasonal movement of animals from one region to another.
12. **Apex predator:** a predator at the top of a food chain, not preyed upon by other animals.
13. **Exoskeleton:** a hard external skeleton that provides support and protection for some animals, such as insects and crustaceans.
14. **Venomous:** capable of injecting venom into another animal through a bite or sting.
15. **Pathogen:** a microorganism that can cause disease in its host.
16. **Vocalization:** the production of sounds for communication purposes.
17. **Incubation:** the process of keeping eggs warm to facilitate hatching.
18. **Concave:** having a surface that curves inward, like the inside of a bowl or spoon.

Ways you can help animals:

Hey there, nature lovers! Want to help our animal friends and their homes? Here are some fun ways you can do it:

1. **Plant Pretty Flowers:** Let's plant some flowers in our garden! When we pick native flowers, like the ones that grow naturally where we live, we give animals yummy food to eat and cozy places to hide.

2. **Pick Up Trash:** When we're outside playing, let's keep an eye out for any trash lying around. By picking it up and throwing it away, we make sure our animal buddies have clean and safe homes. Always ask an adult for help!

3. **Make Homes for Animals:** We can build special homes for animals right in our backyard! How about making a little pond for frogs or a birdhouse for our feathered friends? They'll love having a cozy place to hang out.

4. **Use Water Wisely:** When we use less water, we help keep rivers and lakes nice and full for animals to drink from and swim in. So, let's turn off the tap when we're not using it and take quick showers like superheroes!

5. **Learn About Cool Animals:** Did you know some animals are in danger of disappearing forever? Let's learn about them and how we can help save them and their homes. We can read books or watch videos together to become animal-saving experts!

By doing these fun things, we can be nature heroes and make sure our animal pals have happy homes to live in! Ready to get started? Let's go save the day!

If you liked this book, you might love Cakes for Snakes!

Available at Amazon, Barnes and Noble, and local bookstores!

**Are you ready for a wild adventure with your favorite animal?
Here's a super fun writing activity just for you:**

1. Pick Your Animal Pal: Choose your most-loved animal friend or find a cool picture of one to inspire your story. Will it be a fierce lion, a playful dolphin, or a mysterious jungle gorilla?

2. Imagine Your Adventure: Picture an awesome adventure for your animal buddy. Are you diving deep into the ocean, soaring high in the sky, or trekking through a dense jungle? Let your imagination run wild!

3. Meet Some Cool Characters: Think up some awesome characters for your story. Maybe your animal meets a wise old owl, a mischievous monkey, or a friendly fish who needs help. Who will join your adventure?

4. Plan Your Epic Journey: What challenges will your animal face along the way? Will they solve a mystery, find a hidden treasure, or save their friends from danger? Think about all the exciting things that could happen!

5. Write Your Story: Grab your pencil and paper and start writing your adventure! Describe the sights, sounds, and smells of your journey. Make it as thrilling and magical as you want!

6. Draw Your Adventure: After you've written your story, it's time to bring it to life with drawings! Sketch your animal hero, the other characters, and the amazing places they visit. Let your creativity shine!

7. Share Your Tale: Once your story and drawings are done, share them with your friends and family! Read your adventure aloud, act it out with stuffed animals, or create a mini-book to show off your awesome tale!

So, are you ready to embark on an amazing animal adventure? Visit www.pandamoniumpublishing.com for more activities!

Did you know?

1. Octopus have three hearts and blue blood. Two of their hearts pump blood to their gills, while the third circulates it to the rest of their body.

2. Honeybees communicate through dance movements known as the "waggle dance" to inform their hive mates about the location of food sources.

3. Elephants are the only mammals that can't jump. Despite their size and strength, their anatomy doesn't allow them to perform this action.

4. Platypuses are one of the few mammals that lay eggs instead of giving birth to live young. They also have venomous spurs on their hind legs.

5. The tongue of a blue whale can weigh as much as an elephant and is large enough for a human to stand on!

Color the octopus!

About the Author

Meet the author, Lacey L. Bakker! Lacey loves all types of animals and learning about them. She has some cool pets like a Mexican Red-Knee Tarantula named Octo-Miss Prime and an American *Rottweiler named Luna. She's had many pets over the years including 2 cats named Simba and Seabass, and a hamster named John McClane (named after the main character in her favorite movie!). When she's not hanging out with her furry friends, Lacey enjoys exploring new places, watching sports, traveling, and going on exciting adventures. Through her stories, she wants to share her love for animals and hopes to inspire others to learn more about them and to care for their habitats.

*Here's a Rottweiler fun fact! Rottweilers have a fascinating history and are considered one of the oldest breeds because they are descendants from drover dogs used by the Roman legions. After the Roman Empire, they played a vital role as working dogs, pulling butcher's meat carts to market and safeguarding the precious cargo. These loyal companions even wore pouches around their necks to protect the money earned by the butchers so that it would not be stolen by thieves!